Worship Feast

Complete Worship Outlines for Lent and Easter

Abingdon Press
Nashville

MANUFACTURED IN THE UNITED STATES OF AMERICA

07 08 09 10 11 12 13 14 15 17—10 9 8 7 6 5 4 3 2 1

COVER DESIGN: KEELY MOORE

Contents

Meet the Writers

Perhaps because he works in Texas and went to College in North Carolina (Duke University), the **Rev. Mike Baughman** is a yankee who can say "y'all" with a Jersey accent (it's really quite beautiful). He is a United Methodist clergyperson who went to a Presbyterian seminary (Princeton Theological Seminary) and currently serves in extension ministries as the Youth Minister at the Episcopal Church of the Transfiguration in Dallas, TX.

In his last appointment, Mike was lead pastor in launching an "emergent" worship gathering, called *veritas* . . . . He has been incredibly blessed to pursue his desire for passionate worship through his formation in such diverse settings for worship.

He enjoys leading workshops and consulting with churches as they plan or re-vision alternative and traditional worship gatherings. He usually gets the most out of worship when he can hear his wife and three kids singing along.

Jenny Youngman has worked and worshiped with youth for ten years. She is the creator of the WORSHIP FEAST series for youth groups, and she is passionate about creative worship. Jenny leads workshops and and worship gatherings for youth retreats and youth worker events. She lives with her family outside of Nashville, TN.

Special thanks to Crys Zinkiewicz for writing the Starters and Josh Tinley for contributing to the WORSHIP FEAST LENT AND EASTER CD.

The Meaning of Lent

You must be strange, or at least a bit weird. I say that because you're actually reading the introduction! Most people will pick up this book and instantly begin trolling for ideas—hunting for a nugget of creativity that can be exploited and built upon in the hope of making an awesome night that ends in teary eyes, group hugs, and lots of people saying, "Thank you, Jesus." (I feel the need, at this point, to totally admit that I've trolled countless books for ideas to exploit in the hopes of crafting just such a night.) Most people will not focus too much on the history or the story. Most will not be all that interested in what the authors have to say about the book.

But that's not you. You're different. You're a little bit weird. And I'm thrilled that you are—because I am too.

If you're reading this introduction, you may be a part of a new movement in youth ministry that is no longer content with pizza parties and entertainment-driven lock-ins. You may be longing for mission trips that lead to lasting change in your youth. You may desire for your students to choose careers that are determined by a sense of calling and vocation rather than lucrative rewards or prestige.

And I'm also thrilled that you are weird, because the first youth ministers in the church were like you too. They needed their new and old members to be reminded of the depth of God's love for them. Likewise they longed for their congregations to be full of disciples whose love of God grew continually deeper. And so they developed a new season in the church year—a time of submission, growth, and giving—called Lent.

Why Submit?
The goal of Lent has always been to strengthen one's identity in Christ, the church, and the Kingdom. During the time that Lent first appeared on the Christian calendar,

followers of Jesus lived in the fierce culture and government of the Roman Empire. Caesar was the lord. Violence was the usual means to enforce his commands, and the subjects of Rome lived accordingly. The church, however, believes that those who are baptized become a part of a new kingdom—the kingdom of God—with Jesus as Lord. Unlike the lordship of Caesar that ruled with violence, strength, and fear, the lordship of Jesus was built upon peace, vulnerability, and hope. The church had to train and re-train its members to think, act, and live in a new way.

In writing this book we have attempted to keep as close as possible to the goals of the early church founders' Lenten goals. Lent should be about helping youth to understand what it means to know God as "Lord." Our contemporary society is far removed from the early church in which the concept of lordship dominated every sphere of life. The Lenten experiences in this book are meant to help church members better understand what it means to be a part of the kingdom of God that submits itself to Christ.

For many of your youth, this will be a radically new concept. Our society is surprisingly submission free—especially when it comes to the church. We live in a church that tends to make membership as easy as possible. Most youth have never been asked to offer themselves—in practical ways—before God. The resources in this book seek to equip you with tools to challenge and inspire your youth in new ways.

Why WORSHIP FEAST?
The early church was creative in the way it accomplished its goals. Long before projection screens and Microsoft Power Point®, the Lenten experience of the people was enhanced by multisensory learning. Hunger, by means of various fasting restrictions, was used to remind the

people how much God provides for them and how much God suffered for them. Some churches began Lent by using salt to make the sign of the cross on the foreheads of those who hoped to join the church and enter into holy preparation. The salt was meant to remind the church of the way that learning can season and preserve those who follow God. Songs and sermons tantalized the ear while water, bread, wine, oil, mucus, and bad breath engaged the senses of touch, taste, and smell. The early church was made up of brilliant educators who knew that the deepest understanding and experience of God came through multisensory learning.

WORSHIP FEAST: COMPLETE WORSHIP OUTLINES FOR LENT AND EASTER is designed to remain within the multisensory spirit of Lent. The worship gatherings and music are meant to stir the soul through more than ordinary means. Each service is meant to be contextualized for your particular group. Use all the bells and whistles (we do literally use bells, but I don't think we used whistles) that will work for you and ignore the rest. Be as elaborate or simple as you are prayerfully called to be. Know that the creativity you bring to the process of leading your teens through the spiritual journey of Lent is a part of our church's ancient faith tradition.

What Can Lent Do?
Lent can and should be nothing short of a life-changing experience. It is the careful work and submission of Lent that empowers us to share in a magnificent new birth on Easter. Through attentively submitting ourselves to God, we journey with Jesus, walk with Jesus, talk with him, weep with him, wonder with him, die with him, and rise again with him. In ten years of youth ministry, I've consistently seen youth get as much out of Lent as they put in—and how much the youth have invested has generally been dictated by how much I plan for and invite them to experience God during this holy time.

Lent is my busiest time of the year. Our youth group has an event almost every day in Holy Week to prepare ourselves for Easter. This past year I even invited youth and their parents to skip school and work on Good Friday to spend the day with me in our downtown area—reflecting on the stations of the cross, joining in various worship services, and participating in different prayer exercises. In the evening we had a lock-in that focused on understanding the theological significance of Good Friday that makes it just as important as Christmas and Easter in the life of the church. All of this time together led to Easter experiences that changed lives.

Why Is Lent So Powerful?
After thoroughly enjoying *The Lord of the Rings* movies and video games, one of my youth convinced me to read the books (moment of confession: I think I skipped the introduction). In these stories there are ancient, moving trees called Ents. At one point, two small creatures called Hobbits (by the names of Merry and Pippen) asks one of the Ent-leaders his name. The ancient tree's response was that, in his language, his name takes too long to say—that isn't like a story.

The story of Jesus' journey to the cross is not a simple one—nor should it be. The story of Jesus' triumph over death does not make sense—it loses its power, beauty, and challenge—when it is divorced from the story of how Jesus ended up in the tomb in the first place. The ancient Ent reluctantly gives Merry and Pippen a short name to call him—Treebeard; yet there is a certain sadness that his full name cannot be expressed.

We have come up with a short name for what happened to Jesus during Holy Week and for what it means to follow Jesus as our Lord. This resource is an effort to give you tools with which to tell the *whole* story of what it means to live into the kingdom of God. It is our hope, goal, and prayer that, through these activities, liturgies, and songs, you might be able to better engage your youth into the full story of the new kingdom into which God calls us. If any story is worth taking a long time to say and listen to—it's this one.

～ ～

So What Does the Word *Lent* Mean?

It never fails. Every time I talk about Lent with any youth group, someone who believes him or herself to be the wittiest person on the planet (and I can usually tell who it will be) raises his or her hand and asks: "Do you mean we're going to have a party to celebrate that stuff in the dryer? I've got some in my belly button right now!" (Based on the sense of humor of most of the youth workers I know, I'm pretty sure that 95 percent of all professional youth workers were the ones who made that joke in their youth group, and 93 percent of all youth workers still make that joke in their youth group. I personally have refrained from making the joke since I graduated from high school—not because I'm above such comments, but so that a new generation of disciples for Jesus Christ can make these witty discoveries of humor.) The word *lent* comes from old English/German words for *spring*. Lent, although often uncomfortably painful and difficult, is given the name for new hope and new life. While it may not be easy, a faithful approach to Lent has the opportunity to bring about incredible new life!

—Mike Baughman

～ ～

How to Use Worship Feast Lent and Easter

A Guide to Services of Submission
This is a collection of worship services and ideas for the entire season of Lent. You can do all of them or just a few, or even mix up the ideas to do your own thing. The theme of the services focuses on submission and how we can live out our submission to the will of Christ. Creativity and the invitation of the Holy Spirit are key to making these services come alive for your group.

We encourage you to describe this experience to your youth as a pilgrimage to the heart of God—that in this Lenten season you will focus on worshiping God with all of your heart, soul, mind, and strength. Invite your students to a journey of submission during Lent and allow God to fill their hearts with love for them.

A Guide to Palm Sunday and Easter Sunrise
The two Sunday services appear on pages 50–56. Typically children process into the sanctuary on Palm Sunday. Let that processional be a "praise party" in worship as the youth lead the Scripture reading and worship music.

Often times youth groups plan and lead the sunrise service on Easter morning. The service included in this resource is a vigil service that can be held either late Saturday night or at sunrise on Easter morning.

A Guide to the Starters

Included on pages 57–59 are short "starters" for Sunday school, youth group, or other gatherings that bring your attention to the Lenten season. The prayers are meant to supplement your group meeting times. Ask different students to lead them each week and let them be a time of centering. Light a candle as you say the prayer, and invite the living Christ to be your Lord.

A Guide to Worship Feast Songs

In the back of this book is a CD that includes five original songs for worship during Lent. You can make copies of the CD for your youth to listen to and learn the songs. The book also includes chords and lyrics for the songs beginning on page 60. Feel free to make copies of these for your student musicians.

Throughout the book, there are suggested songs, but feel free to add others or to add more group singing to the services.

Get to know these songs, and through them, let your hearts worship the living Christ. They were written especially for your group and for this special Lenten season.

Submitting to God

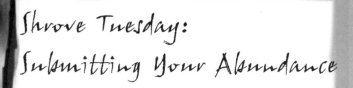

Shrove Tuesday: Submitting Your Abundance

Goal: To be freed from the burden of sin and submit everything we have to God.

Scripture: *"Jesus said to him, 'If you wish to be perfect, go, sell your possessions, and give the money to the poor, and you will have treasure in heaven; then come, follow me.' When the young man heard this word, he went away grieving, for he had many possessions"* (Matthew 19:21–22).

How the Youth Will Engage God:
Shrove Tuesday is historically the day on which Christians confess their sins and celebrate with a feast to use up the foods not allowed during the Lenten fast. Because it was customary to not eat milk, eggs, meats, and fats during Lent, early Christians would make fried pancakes and doughnuts to use up these items.

The celebration, sometimes called "Mardi Gras" or "Fat Tuesday," is another way of saying, "eating the fats to be abstained from during Lent." Today different churches celebrate this day in a variety of ways.

Help your youth experience God by confessing your sins together and celebrating a feast before beginning a Lenten fast.

Supplies:
Note cards with written statements

The Feast:

1. Host a pancake party. Recruit parents to cook and serve a feast. Plan to play the WORSHIP FEAST LENT AND EASTER CD as background music. Ahead of time, prepare note cards on which are printed the incomplete statements below. Place one card on each seat:

✳ Lord, I confess _____ .

✳ Lord, I have so much. I'll give it all to you by

_____ .

2. Invite the students to reflect on the statements, even as they feast at the table. When everyone has finished eating, move to a different space for a closing worship time. Remind students to bring their cards.

The Service:

1. Gather together around an empty table to contrast the abundant buffet you just enjoyed. Focus on the act of confession and submitting to God all that we are in all of our abundance. Sing together the "Jesus Prayer" from the CD in the back of this book.

2. Read aloud the passage from Matthew, then pause for a few minutes of silence. Hand out pens or pencils and invite the students to complete the statements on their cards.

3. Sing together "Worship You" from the CD in the back of this book. As you sing, invite students to lay their cards on the table as an act of submitting their individual abundance for God's use. Invite a student to close in prayer.

Ash Wednesday: Submitting Your Voice

Goal: To experience silence as an act of submitting your voices to God.

Scripture: *"O LORD, my heart is not lifted up, my eyes are not raised too high; I do not occupy myself with things too great and too marvelous for me. But I have calmed and quieted my soul"* (Psalm 131:1-2a).

Instructions:
Prepare an altar table using fabric, candles, crosses, and a few icon prints. Gather youth around the table, preferably sitting on the floor. If your church already offers an Ash Wednesday service that includes the imposition of ashes, you may want to lead this service with your youth at a different time during the day. If your church has an evening service, meet with your students before or right after school. If your church does not hold an Ash Wednesday service and you want to include the imposition of ashes into the following service, add it to the closing.

∼ The Prayer Service ∼

Explain to youth that you will sing together and read some Scriptures before pausing for a time of silence, during which they are encouraged to seek God. Remind them that it is not necessary to "think" their prayers as if they were praying aloud; instead encourage them to be still in the silence of God's presence. Suggest that they offer to God the items or actions they feel led to give up during Lent.

Sing Together:
* ☀ "Jesus Prayer"
* ☀ "Carry Your Cross" (Both songs are from the CD in the back of this book.)

Read the Scriptures:
1. Ask a volunteer to read aloud **Psalm 131:1-2a**.

2. Say: "Calm and quiet your soul, putting aside every other thought for now. Take the next few minutes and settle into the silence. When you hear the psalm again, meditate on whatever words jump out at you. When you hear the passage for a third time, allow God to speak to you and truly listen to what God may be saying to you."

3. Read aloud the psalm twice more with five to ten minutes of silence between each reading.

4. Say: "Today is Ash Wednesday, a day we mark as the beginning of our journey to the cross—the beginning of Lent. Today we submit our journey to God. Today we begin our Lenten fast. What will you give up or take on to focus on your walk with God? Hold that commitment in your heart as we sing together again." Sing "Doxology" (from the CD in the back of this book).

5. Close in prayer.

Lent Week 1:
Submitting Our Devotion

Goal: To help students maintain a disciplined prayer life during Lent.

Scripture: *"Be cheerful no matter what; pray all the time; thank God no matter what happens. This is the way God wants you who belong to Christ Jesus to live"* (1 Thessalonians 5:17, THE MESSAGE).

How the Youth Will Engage God:
Long before people were giving up soda and candy for Lent, Christians were devoting themselves to extra prayer time during the Lenten season. This week the youth will create individual sets of prayer beads. Prayer beads have a long history in the Eastern Orthodox tradition. Although similar to a rosary in that it uses beads to encourage prayer, it is different in that the prayers are simpler and intent upon confession.

The youth will pray as they create the prayer beads, then learn to pray as they walk, as they eat, as they talk, and as they live. They can even pray in class. This week is filled with prayer that leads to prayer that leads to prayer that leads to a deeper relationship with God.

The tone of this prayer activity will vary with your group and how you decide to lead it. If students are able to choose their individual beads, there will be more energy and therefore noise as they begin to express their creativity. As they enter the construction phase, encourage youth to focus more on praying the prayers than on conversation with those around them. Eventually youth may notice while praying individually that they are surrounded by many voices muttering prayers. This collective praying can be a very powerful experience!

Supplies:
Provide the following materials for each youth participating. If you have enough time, youth may sort their own beads. If you are limited on time, sort the beads ahead of time so that each youth receives a set of beads and a cord. The beads on any one chain should match because each represents the same prayer.

* 56 beads / chain
* 3 metallic beads or dividers / chain
* 1 cross or other religious charm
* 18 inches of hemp line or other sturdy cord for stringing

Instructions:
1. Allow time for youth to relax together before taking a set of beads and claiming their individual space in the room. (If youth are choosing their own beads/charms/dividers, include time to do so before they move to their individual spaces.) Give youth some historical background on the beads they will construct.

2. Say: "You are about to make a Chotki. Chotkis come from the Eastern Orthodox Church tradition. They are a tool to help us pray more often. By praying more, we give more of our devotion to God, especially during this Lenten season.

"As you make your Chotki, you will pray. A prayer is associated with each individual bead. As you string a bead onto the cord, say its appropriate prayer. Your supply sheet will remind you about the order of the beads and what to pray." (See page 24 for supply list.)

3. Continue: "The first prayer is the Jesus Prayer, and you will pray this prayer the most. Say, 'Lord Jesus Christ, Son of God, have mercy on me, a sinner.' If you like, you may even add the rhythm of your breath to the prayer."

> < breathe in > "Lord Jesus Christ, Son of God,"
> < breathe out > "Have mercy on me, a sinner."

Add: "In this way, you breathe in the presence of Christ and breathe out your confession and sins.

"After you have prayed this fourteen times (which is twice the number of wholeness in the Hebrew tradition), you will add a divider to your beads as a prompt to pray the Lord's Prayer. When you have strung all of your beads and all of your dividers, you will tie off your cord and attach a charm on the end. Then you will recite the Apostles' Creed."

4. Play background music as the youth make their Chotkis. When you notice that youth are nearly finished, continue with the following instructions.

5. Say: "Now that you've completed your Chotki, I challenge you to use it. Keep it in a pocket. Wrap it around your wrist. Take it with you to school, to the doctor's office, to church. Use it as a reminder to pray as often as possible.

"Some people who regularly use a Chotki discover that the Jesus Prayer, the Lord's Prayer, and the Apostles' Creed eventually begin to loop over and over in their minds—even when they are thinking about other things. However, it isn't a distraction; instead it is a reminder of God's presence, love, and mercy. This continual prayer thought, people believe, is what it means to 'pray without ceasing,' offering up to God constant and complete devotion." Close by leading your group to do the full Chotki aloud and in unison.

6. Follow up with the youth by occasionally e-mailing to ask if they are using their Chotkis. Encourage them to set goals for themselves (like saying it once a day throughout Lent, or doing it one more time a day each day until they are saying it forty times a day). Those who purposefully use the Chotkis discover that it is much easier to regularly practice than they first believed.

CHOTKIS

Bead Order
- 14 Beads, 1 Divider
- 14 Beads, 1 Divider
- 14 Beads, 1 Divider
- 14 Beads, Tie off the string and attach cross to excess line.

THE PRAYERS

REGULAR BEAD = JESUS PRAYER

< inhale > *Lord Jesus Christ, Son of God,*
< exhale > *Have mercy on me a sinner.*

DIVIDERS = THE LORD'S PRAYER

Our Father in heaven,
hallowed be your name,
your kingdom come,
your will be done, on earth as in heaven.
Give us this day our daily bread.
And forgive us our trespasses,
as we forgive those who trespass against us.
And lead us not into temptation,
but deliver us from evil.
For thine is the kingdom, and the power,
and the glory, forever. Amen.

CROSS / KNOT = APOSTLES' CREED

*I believe in God, the Father Almighty,
creator of heaven and earth.*

*And in Jesus Christ, his only Son, our Lord,
who was conceived by the Holy Spirit,
born of the Virgin Mary,
suffered under Pontius Pilate,
was crucified, died, and was buried;
he descended to the dead.
On the third day he rose again;
he ascended into heaven,
is seated at the right hand of the Father,
and will come again to judge the living and the dead.*

*I believe in the Holy Spirit,
the holy catholic* church,
the communion of saints,
the forgiveness of sins,
the resurrection of the body
and the life everlasting. Amen.*

*catholic with a little "c" means "universal"

Lent Week 1

Lent Week 2: Submitting Our Work

Goal: To offer our work to God.

Scripture: *"Let the favor of the Lord our God be upon us, and prosper for us the work of our hands—O prosper the work of our hands!"* (Psalm 90:17).

How the Youth Will Engage God:
Permanent markers will be used as an object lesson to help participants commit their work to God. The temporary nature of "permanent" markers will prompt discussion.

Supplies:
Permanent markers, candles or pen lights

Instructions:
1. Give each participant a permanent marker (do not use yellow or other light colors that won't be visible on skin) and a candle or pen light.

2. Instruct students to find a prayerful space. They may sit, stand, or lie down.

3. Ask the group to use the candle or pen light to look at their hands. Say, "Our hands can say a lot about us and what we do." Ask youth for initial observations of their hands.

4. After listening to initial observations, encourage the youth to silently reflect on the following questions. Pause for a full minute or more after each question.

 ✳ Are your hands dry or rough or wrinkled or smooth?
 ✳ Are your hands strong from use or soft from protection?
 ✳ If a stranger looked at your hands, what might he or she think that you do with your hands?
 ✳ Do you like your hands?

5. Say: "Hands are symbols for the work we do. We all use our hands in our professions—to carry things, to turn pages, to write with a pen, to pull levers. Some of us use our hands more than others. Often times we separate our work or school lives from our lives with God, but God wants every part of us. Our work is one of the most important things that we do. When we submit our work to God, we increase our devotion to God through the very things we do and learn."

6. Ask the group to reflect on the following questions. Pause briefly after reading aloud each question.

 ✳ How does your work—what you do for school, for chores, for money—serve the kingdom of God?
 ✳ Does something about your work need to change so that the task can be offered for the service of God?

✷ Are you willing to devote the work of your hands and mind to God?

7. Instruct the youth to take their permanent markers and write the word "GOD'S" on the palms of their hands.

8. Say: "Even though you are using permanent markers, the letters will quickly fade. We frequently make decisions to offer ourselves to God and believe that these decisions are permanent. In reality, both the marks on our hands and the decisions we make for God must be made again and again. Spend some time looking at God's name written on your hands—the symbol for your work—and pray that God can use your work for the glory of God's kingdom."

9. After pausing for some time to reflect, close by saying aloud together A Covenant Prayer in the Wesleyan Tradition (see the following page).

A COVENANT PRAYER IN THE
WESLEYAN TRADITION

I am no longer my own, but thine.
Put me to what thou wilt, rank me with whom thou wilt.
Put me to doing, put me to suffering.
Let me be employed by thee or laid aside for thee,
exalted for thee or brought low for thee.
Let me be full, let me be empty.
Let me have all things, let me have nothing.
I freely and heartily yield all things to thy pleasure
and disposal.
And now, O glorious and blessed God,
Father, Son, and Holy Spirit,
thou art mine, and I am thine. So be it.
And the covenant which I have made on earth,
let it be ratified in heaven. Amen.

Lent Week 3: Submitting Our Petitions

Goal: To give students a deeper sense of God's desire to meet our needs.

Scripture: *"Ask, and you will receive. Search, and you will find. Knock, and the door will be opened for you. Everyone who asks will receive. Everyone who searches will find. And the door will be opened for everyone who knocks. Would any of you give your hungry child a stone, if the child asked for some bread? Would you give your child a snake if the child asked for a fish? As bad as you are, you still know how to give good gifts to your children. But your heavenly Father is even more ready to give good things to people who ask"* (Matthew 7:7-11, CEV).

Supplies:
Washable markers, paper, large container of water (such as a child's backyard pool or several cooking pans with deep sides). *Optional:* Water pump (If you use a small water pump from a home fountain and set it up in the corner of your water container, it will provide additional motion and sound.); incense sticks provide an additional visual effect.

Instructions:
1. Give each participant paper and a washable marker.

2. Light the incense stick(s) if you're using them.

3. Say: "One of the most common and important aspects of prayer is asking God for the things we need. Today we will offer up to God our needs and desires."

4. Read aloud **Matthew 7:7-11**.

5. Say: "Jesus asks us to submit ourselves to God, but God is not an insensitive tyrant. God cares about our needs. We cannot offer our whole selves to God without offering our desires, needs, hopes, and dreams. Tear your piece of paper into four sections. On one section, write your needs. On the second, write your dreams for the future. On another write your desires. On the fourth section, write other gifts, attitudes, actions, feelings, and so on that you want to offer to God. Take your time and be honest as you write or draw pictures or symbols of your petitions."

6. Allow time for students to write, then say: "When you have finished your lists, go to the water and place your papers into the water. Watch what happens and spend time praying to God." Pray silently for the youth as they submit their petitions to God.

Closing Prayer:
Pray together A Covenant Prayer in the Wesleyan Tradition (see page 27).

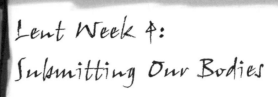

Lent Week 4:
Submitting Our Bodies

Goal: To give students a deeper sense of how they devote their physical beings to God.

Scripture: *"You shall love the Lord your God with all your heart, and with all your soul, and with all you mind, and with all your strength"* (Mark 12:30).

Supplies:
Crosses, icons, Trinity symbols—items to use as a focal point. The items need not be fancy, but they should be large enough for people to see.

Instructions:
1. Invite each student to find a comfortable space in the room that is near the object that most reminds him or her of God. It may be one of the items displayed or it may be a cross necklace or other personal object they have with them in class.

2. Say: "When we serve God, we use more than just our minds. We submit our belief to God, but Jesus asks for more—he also wants our bodies. We cannot serve the poor or lovingly care for family, neighbors, or friends using only our minds. God asks us to submit out whole selves. Praying is a spiritual *and* physical experience.

"In some faith traditions, Christians kneel when they pray the prayer of confession. Do you know why?

(Wait for answers.) Some congregations stand when the Scriptures are read or while Communion is being prepared. Why do you think people stand during those moments? What does it mean to stand up for something?" (Wait for answers.)

Continue: "Today we're going to use prayer postures as a way of submitting our bodies to God. Often when we are extremely stressed or upset, our bodies can become uncomfortable, and then our bodies can affect our mind. Also, when we're sick or hurt, our emotions are affected. Our posture can signal to our brains and our souls the way we approach God.

"Most of us know at least one prayer position—hands folded, head down, and eyes closed. What does this posture say about our relationship with God?"

∼ Prayer Posture 1 ∼

1. Say: "Kneel in front of the object you chose as a symbol of God. Extend your hands forward with palms up. Tilt your head up, keeping your eyes fixed on the object. Before praying, reflect on the following questions. (Pause briefly after reading aloud each one.)

* How do you feel as you kneel in this position?
* How do you think these feelings might affect how you pray?

2. Read aloud **Matthew 16:24-26.**

* What do you have to offer God that you are currently holding back?

✳ In giving your whole self over to God, what does God offer you?

3. Close with a personal prayer or: *"Lord God, we give and receive from you. Help our desires to decrease so that your will and life through us might increase. Amen."*

～ Prayer Posture 2 ～

1. Say: "The second prayer position is one of submission. For this position you will need to get on your knees and lean forward. Place your forehead on the floor (or as close to it as possible, depending on how flexible you are) and stretch your arms out in front of you. If this position is too uncomfortable for you to maintain for the next few minutes (due to knee or back injuries), then you may alternatively lie face-down on the floor. Turn your body so that you are pointing towards the object that reminds you of God. Reflect on the following questions." (Pause briefly after reading aloud each question.)

✳ How do you feel as you kneel/lie in this position?
✳ How do you think these feelings might affect how you pray?

2. Read aloud **James 4:6-10**.

✳ What does it mean for you to submit to God?
✳ What, in your life, is more important than God?

3. Pray: *"Loving Lord, we lie here exposed and humble before you. Take our humility and build something new in the name of the Father and of the Son and of the Holy Spirit. Amen."*

⚰ Prayer Posture 3 ⚰

1. Say: "Now it's time to rest. Lie on your back and place your arms by your sides or fold your hands across your torso and relax." Ask: "How do you feel? How will these feelings affect the way you pray?"

2. Read aloud **Deuteronomy 5:14-15.**

3. Say: "The Lord does not demand that we work for God's kingdom without resting. Keeping a sabbath, or resting, keeps us close to God. Where, in your life, do you need rest?" Pause briefly as students reflect.

4. Pray: *"God of rest and calm, you created the sabbath for us. Help us to remember the importance of rest. We ask that we might rest in your loving arms. Amen."*

Closing:
1. Say: "These prayer postures represent our journey with God. First, we receive God's gifts. Then we submit our lives to the God who makes our paths straight. Lastly, we rest in the presence of God.

"Pay attention to your body as you continue to pray throughout Lent. Try out different ways of positioning your body. If you feel like your relationship with God is out of balance—try standing on one foot while you pray. If you feel like you need God to take you somewhere new, pray while jogging or riding your bike. Use your whole body as you pray."

Lent Week 5: Submitting Our Possessions

Goal: Empower youth to use the gifts they have for the good of the Kingdom.

Scripture: *"The servant who knows what his master wants and ignores it, or insolently does whatever he pleases, will be thoroughly thrashed. But if he does a poor job through ignorance, he'll get off with a slap on the hand. Great gifts mean great responsibilities; greater gifts, greater responsibilities!"* (Luke 12:48, THE MESSAGE)

How the Youth Will Engage God:
Youth will examine the items in their pockets, purses, or backpacks to see what they have that they can use to build God's kingdom.

Instructions:
1. Encourage participants to find a prayerful space in the meeting room.

2. Ask students to place on the floor in front of themselves the contents of their pockets/purses/backpacks. If they carry wallets, they should also empty the wallets so that the contents are visible.

3. Say: "You have received many gifts. Whether or not you feel that you have earned those gifts, all

things come from God and by God's grace. You were born into a wealthy nation. The poorest of our country are rich by most other countries' standards.

"God is our Lord and King. In the days of kings, a king owned everything within his kingdom and could claim the property held by anyone who resided there. If you have claimed Jesus as your Lord, then you are called to submit your possessions to God.

"Look at the items in front of you. These items are always at your disposal. Inside the pockets of your pants, purses, and bags, you have overwhelming access to finances, communication, information, knowledge, and transportation—access of which previous generations could only dream!"

4. Read aloud **Luke 12:48**.

5. Say: "Spend the next fifteen minutes examining each of the objects in front of you. Ask yourself, 'How can I use the ability represented by this item for the glory of God's kingdom?'"

6. Close by saying in unison A Covenant Prayer in the Wesleyan Tradition (see page 27).

Holy Week: Maundy Thursday
Submitting Our Surprise

Goal: To help youth imagine the disciples' perspective on the Last Supper and to gain a glimpse of Jesus' submission to God.

This worship service is designed to take place the Thursday before Easter (usually in the evening). It is meant to convey to youth the emotions and power felt by those who gathered on this night for the Last Supper.

Scripture:
"After sunset [Jesus] came with the Twelve. As they were at the supper table eating, Jesus said, 'I have something hard but important to say to you: One of you is going to hand me over to the conspirators, one who at this moment is eating with me'" (Mark 14:12-42 17-18, THE MESSAGE).

How the Youth Will Engage God:
Youth will experience taste, conversation, movement from one place to another, and storytelling.

Supplies:
A light snack for the gathering time, bread or rolls and juice for Communion, tables and chairs, candles for tables, Communion chalices, tablecloths, flowers, other decorations that may help set the mood and enhance the service, and printed copies of any prayers or liturgy that your priest or pastor may use

Instructions:

1. Decide upon an initial gathering place, remembering that you will not stay there very long. In another room, set up tables and chairs to seat 12 or 13 people each. On each table set out food and drinks for the snack. Set the bread and juice for Communion in the center of the tables.

2. Contact ahead of time those who will assume leadership roles during the worship service and give them the necessary information and instructions. Also make sure they have copies of the script prior to the service. Enlist the following leaders:

Host: The host will introduce the service and help participants to transition smoothly from one part to the next. He or she should also make sure the juice and bread for Communion are available on the tables.

Presider: In most mainline traditions, a person who is ordained for sacraments must preside over a proper celebration of Communion. Ask your pastor for suggestions and input about your service.

Song Leader: Enlist a student to lead some WORSHIP FEAST worship songs.

Narrator: The narrator reads aloud Scripture passages that connect the liturgy to the events of the Last Supper. Be sure the reader reads clearly and with passion.

∼ Maundy Thursday Service ∼

GATHERING

HOST: "Welcome! It is wonderful to have you here this evening! Tonight the service will be a little different from our normal style of worship, but I assure you—it *is* a worship service. We will follow the same pattern of worship that has guided the followers of Christ for two thousand years and will open our hearts and minds to the same God.

"I invite you to walk the way of the cross and to allow yourself to be surprised. Part of tonight's purpose is to help us gain a better appreciation of how the disciples would have experienced the Last Supper on the night before Jesus was handed over to the authorities. Because we've heard the story so often, we tend to forget that, at one point in history, none of what took place on that night was yet history. You'll notice that you did not receive an order of service when you entered. The disciples did not have a schedule of what was to happen that night— no set time at which Judas would be revealed as a traitor ... no warning of the anguish that awaited them in the garden. Tonight I invite you to experience the same surprise, the same uncertainty, the same wonder at this incredible God, Man, Lord, Rabbi, and broken, healing Savior who we never quite understand."

Song Leader: "Jesus and the disciples gathered at the Passover Feast for a night of food, prayer, and song. An important part of the singing on Passover is that it tells the story of God's work and invites God to be present. In that spirit, let's sing together." Lead the group in singing "Worship You" from the CD in the back of this book.

PROCLAMATION OF THE WORD

Narrator: Read aloud **Mark 14:12-16**.

Host: "As we gather around the table and feast, let us join with one another, the disciples, the saints of all generations, and with Jesus. Have a seat, enjoy the food, enjoy the conversation, and wait—with great anticipation—for what might happen on this holy night.

(*Encourage the youth to be seated at the tables. Allow 10–15 minutes for people to enjoy the snacks on the table and to relax while talking with one another. As they sit and eat, ask a few people to circulate, making sure that people are comfortable and have whatever they need.*)

Narrator: (*with very little warning to the group, so that some may even miss part of what you say*) Read aloud **Mark 14:17-21**.

After reading, the narrator should promptly sit down without giving any further instruction. There may be an awkward silence as people wait. This is OK and intended. Wait five minutes before beginning the next section.

RESPONSE TO THE WORD

PRESIDER: (*interrupting*) "We ask forgiveness from God for the ways we have fallen short of God's call upon our lives. We join with the generations of those who have celebrated the Passover Feast by giving thanks for God's delivering grace. May God grant you peace, forgiveness, and grace. Amen.

"I'd like to ask someone at each table to help me as I lead us in celebrating Communion. Use the bread and juice on the tables and follow my actions."

(*Hold up the loaf of bread or roll that is left on the table, indicating that someone at each table should do the same.*)

"While they were eating, Jesus took the loaf of bread, gave thanks, broke it, and then gave it to the disciples, saying, 'This is my body, which is given for you. Do this in remembrance of me.'"

(*Tear off a piece of bread from the loaf and pass it around your table, indicating that someone from each of the other tables should do the same.*)

"When the supper was over, Jesus did the same with the cup, saying, 'Drink from this, all of you. This is my blood of a new covenant, poured out for you and for many—for the forgiveness of sins. As often as you eat from this bread and drink from this cup, do this in remembrance of me.'"

(*Dip your bread into the cup, pass the cup around your table and eat your bread, again cuing people at the other tables to do the same.*)

NARRATOR: (*Pause till you can see that everyone has received the bread and juice.*) Read aloud **Mark 14:26**.

SONG LEADER: Lead the participants in singing the "Jesus Prayer" and "Doxology."

HOST: "Now we will go outside, not to the Mount of Olives, but (depending on what you have worked out ahead of time) to a garden/cemetery, just as the disciples did. Please stand up."

(*As people stand, encourage them to take coats if needed.*)

NARRATOR: (*Once again, interrupt—as if you missed your earlier cue.*) Read aloud **Mark 14:27-32a**.

After the narrator finishes reading the Scripture, the group should move to their final destination. (A garden or cemetery are ideal locations, but simply going outdoors is fine.)

HOST: (*Once the people have gathered and are silent, say . . .*) "Two thousand years ago, on a night very similar to this . . . in a place similar to this, Jesus spent his last hours with his disciples. Surely the disciples were confused. Few would have suspected or believed, despite Jesus' warnings, that everything would soon be different—forever.

"What we need to remember is that the disciples were just people—people like you and me. They did not expect to follow some rabbi with the light of the divine in his eyes. The disciples weren't all that wise or well-informed or well-off anyway. And here they were, without knowing it, spending their last night with the one person who had truly known them, who had set their world on fire. They are content from food and wine—and they are filled with wonder. And they are tired—incredibly tired."

NARRATOR: Read aloud **Mark 14:32b-41**.

SENDING FORTH

HOST: "All is not well. The cross looms distant on the dark horizon, and the world teeters at the edge of a great fall. May God keep you safe through this night, until we gather tomorrow and continue the passion of our Lord. Amen."

Encourage people to leave in silence.

Holy Week: Good Friday
Stations of the Cross

How the Youth Will Engage God:
The Stations of the Cross represent a pilgrimage to the heart of God—a journey with Christ to the cross. Many schools close on Good Friday, so you might consider a daytime gathering. Or, host a late-night event after your church's Good Friday service.

Instructions:
Set up each station as a separate worship center, and be as creative or simple as you like. Consider displaying images that relate to each station's focus. Youth will walk from station to station in consecutive order, so make sure there is room for one or two students at each station. Lead in a time of singing and prayer before beginning this experience, or close with worship and prayer. Take any or all of these ideas and customize them for your youth.

Supplies:
For each station, you'll need the various supplies from the Tasks, such as candles, icons, crosses, and small tables.

* **Station 1: Judgment at the Hands of Pilate**
  John 19:13-16

Reading: "Jesus suffered at the hands of many for a greater good. When have you

endured hardship for the benefit of others? Jesus was judged by important people who did not understand him, yet he did not correct them. Why? Has God ever called you to be misunderstood?"

Task: Use the pen to write the word *Misunderstood* on the paper. Then, all around the word write one-word descriptions of what it feels like to be misunderstood.

Prayer: "We adore you, O Christ, and we bless you because of the injustice you accept for our sakes. I walk by you this day. Help me to remain by your side and to be faithful, though I have run from you many times before."

✳ Station 2: Jesus Carries His Cross
John 19:17

Reading: "How heavy was the cross? What weight did Jesus carry apart from the weight of the cross? Which was heavier—the spiritual weight or the physical weight? What spiritual weight are you carrying?"

Task: Pick up the weight and hold it for a few minutes. Imagine the physical weight of Jesus' cross. Now imagine the emotional and spiritual weight you carry around everyday. Feel the weight of it.

Prayer: "We adore you, O Christ, and we bless you, because you carried the weight of the world upon your already beaten frame. Grant me the strength to carry on."

✳ Station 3: Jesus Falls
Isaiah 50:6

Reading: "Imagine watching Jesus stumble and fall from the exhaustion and fatigue, being pushed around like a nobody. As he is brought to this low point, you watch with the realization that he is enduring all of that pain for you. Watch him stand up again and keep going. Again, for you."

Task: Fall to the ground and attempt to get up without using your hands or arms. Imagine the pain of simply trying to stand up, with no help and with the weight of a cross on your back.

Prayer: "We adore you, O Christ, and we bless you, for you have endured utter fatigue and have decided again and again to continue. We adore you, O Christ, for you have endured endless excuses for times when we have failed you, yet you persist in loving us. We have pushed you down by adding our weight to your cross. Grant that I may help you carry it and not weigh it down."

✳ Station 5: Simon Helps Carry
the Cross
Luke 23:26

Reading: "His face is tired. He looks at the crowd and notices an outsider. His friends have left him, so he allows this outsider to help. God accepts the help of others! This should be my story. If Christ can accept help, why should I think that I do not need to do the same?"

Task: Write a letter to God as a prayer for help? For what do you need help? Can you be the one to carry a burden for someone else?

Prayer: "We adore you, and we bless you for showing us how to share our burdens with others."

✳ **Station 7: Jesus Falls Again**
   Isaiah 53:4

Reading: "The weight is becoming too much to bear. His body is giving way to the abuse. You look on and wonder in awe, *All of this is for me?*"

Task: Fall to the ground again, and this time, stay there. Feel the weight of your body on the ground, nearly incapable of moving anymore.

Prayer: "We adore you, O Christ, and we bless you. I behold you on the ground—agony taking its toll on your body. Help me to store this image in my heart. I will never feel alone in my suffering while remembering this image of Jesus on the ground."

✳ **Station 9: Jesus Falls a Third Time**
   Mark 15:22-23

Reading: "As Jesus approaches Golgatha, the journey becomes more difficult. Why did Jesus fall this third time? Was it the sight of the hills that weakened his resolve? that weakened his knees? Nothing is left in this frail and broken body—nothing is left in his spirit. Yet, somehow, he stands one more time."

Task: Fall to the ground one last time. Spend a moment feeling the heaviness of your body. Then rise, and as you do, imagine the power of the Spirit lifting you to your feet.

Prayer: "We adore you, O Christ, and we bless your name. I don't understand. You are so weak and broken. How can they do this to you? How can *I* do this to you by denying you over and over? When will I help you rather than hurt you with your cross?"

* **Station 10: Jesus Is Stripped**
   Matthew 27:28

Reading: "Naked—Jesus faces his death. Nothing is hidden from the world. He couldn't be more human in this moment—his body exposed, without shield or cover. He does this for me. Even the insides of his flesh are exposed through the wounds of his back, torso, and arms. It's all there—for the world to see."

Task: Read aloud **Psalm 139:1-6** and try to memorize one verse.

Prayer: "We adore you, O Christ, and we bless your name. Strip away my foolish armor and my desperate fig leaves. Expose me, search me, look even beneath my skin. I know that exposure will hurt; but it will hurt even more if I remain hidden."

✳ Station 11: Jesus Is Nailed to the Cross
Luke 23:34

Reading: "There is so much blood. Every time Jesus lifts up his body to catch a breath, he does so in spite of the nails being hammered into his body. I make myself watch. And I look at his face. He's doing this for me. Can there be any agony of mine he does not feel? My heart overflows with both sadness and gratitude."

Task: Nail your prayers, your thoughts, your sins, your hopes, your affections, and your pain—to the cross. Submit them to Christ.

Prayer: "We adore you, O Christ, and we bless your name. This is for me? I can hardly believe it. I wish I could take it back. I could never ask you to do this for me—yet you have. Help me to accept this gift of great sacrifice."

✳ Station 12: Jesus Dies on the Cross
Mark 15:33-37

Reading: "So this is salvation—our bold, broken, bizarre salvation. His last words echo in my head. I wish I knew what those words meant to him. Is there peace before his final breath?"

Task: Breathe in and out—deliberately and slowly. Feel the oxygen in your mouth, nose, and lungs. This air that you breathe is life.

Prayer: "We adore you, O Christ, and we bless your name. In a way I'm relieved by your death. You no longer have to suffer, yet your final cry echoes in my head and throughout the world. The world groans with you—at least it should. Sadly, most of the world continues as if nothing happened. Help me to hear your cries."

✳ Station 13: Jesus Is Taken Down From the Cross
Luke 23:50-53

Reading: "Jesus' mother holds his lifeless body. I want to touch his body as she does. I want to be held as she holds him. I do not know whether to scream . . . or sigh . . . or sing softly."

Task: Sing or listen to the "Jesus Prayer."

Prayer: "We adore you, O Christ, and we bless your name. You leave blood stains in your wake. I have been stained. The whole world has been stained, yet there is love and there is tenderness. Help me to love. Help me to be tender. Be tender with me."

✳ Station 14: Jesus Is Laid in the Tomb
Matthew 27:59-60

Reading: "What do I do now? It's over."

Task: Draw or paint a picture of the tomb and reflect on its finality.

Prayer: "We adore you, O Christ, and we bless your name. I give thanks to the Lord for the journey along 'the way' of the cross. May my life be worthy of the One who sacrificed everything for me. Come back to us again, Christ Jesus. Help us to always return to you."

Holy Week: Palm Sunday
Submitting Our Praise

Goal: To lead youth in singing and praising God for sending Jesus Christ to save us.

Scripture: *"Hosanna! Blessed is the one who comes in the name of the Lord! Blessed is the coming kingdom of our ancestor David! Hosanna in the highest heaven!"* (Mark 11:9-10)

How the Youth Will Engage God:
Youth will have a praise party for the Christ by singing praise songs and reading Scriptures.

Instructions:
If your congregation has a youth worship band, ask them to play praise songs. If you don't have a band, use the CD in the back of this book and lead youth in singing along.

Read aloud **Mark 11:1-11**, the story of Jesus' triumphal entry into Jerusalem. Then sing some more praise songs and close with this responsive prayer:

LEADER: Jesus, we praise you.
ALL: Hosanna to the King. (*Pause and allow youth to say this phrase after each of the following lines.*)
LEADER: You are the Savior of the world.
LEADER: We cry, "Save us!"
LEADER: We cry, "Forgive us!"
LEADER: We cry, "Holy!"
ALL: Hosanna! Amen.

Holy Week: Easter Vigil
Submitting Our Joy

The Easter Vigil has a long church history. Typically celebrated on either the evening before Easter (Holy Saturday) or sunrise on Easter morning, it is meant to be a worship service of anticipation and exultation as the shimmering light of Christ seeps out from the endless horizon of death.

This service is much like a modern-day wake where friends gather and tell stories of their lost loved one. But this is no ordinary wake—it's extraordinary!

How the Youth Will Engage God:
Youth will experience light changes, auditory sensation, the act of holding and lighting a candle, and the feel of water as a form of celebration.

Supplies:
Candles and bells for everyone; four large candles for four readers; a Paschal candle (or a large, white candle and the supplies to make it a Paschal, see page 55); matches, water for sprinkling

Instructions:
Adjust and tweak these ideas to fit your group. Enlist four good readers to lead the liturgy. They should rehearse the liturgy so that the worship experience flows well. Plan to lead the liturgy in darkness, or near darkness.

Easter Vigil Liturgy

READER 1: "Something strange is happening—there is a great stillness. The whole earth keeps silence because the King is asleep." (*Bell toll; #2 lights her candle.*)

READER 2: What do you do when someone you love dies? Jesus, the perfector of our faith, the chosen one, the Messiah, the one upon whom the hopes of a people ... (*Bell toll; #3 lights her candle.*)

READER 3: The hopes of a nation rests ... (*Bell toll; #1 lights his candle.*)

READER 1: The hopes of a world rest

READER 3: The one to whom we submit our bodies

READER 2: The one to whom we submit our devotion

READER 1: The one to whom we submit our petitions

READER 3: The one to whom we submit our possessions

READER 2: The one to whom we submit our will

READER 1: The one to whom we submit our work

READER 2: (*Pause*) He is dead.

READER 1: In the grave.

READER 2: (*slowly*) And the world rests in silence. (*long pause*)

READER 3: What do you do when someone you love dies? Do you huddle together in silence? Do you let out loud cries that pierce the night that surrounds your heart?

READER 2: Do you weep silently?

READER 1: Do you share stories, calling the deceased to life—if only in our own minds and hearts? (*one bell toll*)

READER 3: Tonight we join with the disciples as they ask questions together, in hiding. (*one bell toll*)

READER 2: Tonight we join with the women as they recall stories while preparing oil and perfume for the body of their Lord. (*one bell toll*)

READER 3: Tonight we join with those who have submitted their lives to this man and watched with horror as he submitted to death. (*one bell toll*)

READER 1: Tonight we join with all the children of God who have walked in the valley of the shadow of death. We walk with those who have longed for green pastures. (*One bell toll; #4 lights his candle.*)

READER 4: And tonight we join with all of creation as we wait anxiously for a new day—a brighter day—an eternal day of newborn hope.

Reader 1: Let us join together in singing. (*Sing together "Carry Your Cross."*)

PROCLAMATION OF THE WORD

READER 1: Sharing stories is one way to grieve at the loss of a loved one. Ancient tradition of Israel holds that telling stories awakens the dead and calls them to life in us, while also awakening the storyteller to remember and hope. Some believe that telling God's stories may even awaken the divine.

READER 2: Candles like the ones you received earlier are used in vigils like ours tonight.

READER 3: We wait with hope for a new day.

READER 4: Vigils are kept to proclaim, with our candles, that light overcomes the deepest darkness.

READER 2: Vigils are a challenge to a world that has walked out on hope.

READER 1: Vigils act as defiance against darkness.

READER 2: As the light fills this room, so may our hope. Each moment carries us closer to the ultimate triumph of God. As the light of the evening grows, so may our joy.

(Ring the bell before each Scripture reading below. If you have access to handbells, invite the handbell director to instruct youth to play the noted chords. While one person reads, the others should walk around and light the congregation members' candles.)

READER 1: Read Job 14:1-14.
READER 2: Read Psalm 22.
READER 3: Read Ezekiel 37:1-14.
READER 4: Read Exodus 14:24–15:1.
(bell toll, note + its third)
READER 2: Read Luke 1:26-38 and 2:1-20.
(bell toll, note + its third)
READER 3: Read Mark 1:1-11
(bell toll, major chord)
READER 1: Matthew 14:13-21. *(bell toll, major chord)*
READER 4: Mark 9:2-8. *(bell toll, major 7th chord)*
READER 2: Mark 14:3-9. *(bell toll, major 7th)*
READER 3: John 1:1-5, 14.

THE PASCHAL CANDLE

(For this section, you can either use a pre-made Paschal candle or make one. To make one, you'll need a large, white candle and some means of writing on the candle, such as a dark crayon, a grease pencil, or a china marker, or cutting into it.)

READER 1: This is our Paschal candle, a light that represents the return of the light of Christ into the world and remembers the cross that brought us to this point. *(Etch a cross on one side of the candle.)*

Christ is the Alpha and Omega—the beginning and the end. *(Etch Alpha and Omega A Ω on the candle.)*

The wick represents Jesus' human nature—the flame represents Jesus' divine nature. Neither can burn without the other.

(Building enthusiasm and volume) The world has lain in waiting, the time of joy is upon us. The hope of the world is here. The God who was born of the womb is now born from the tomb. We who have shared in his death, now share in his life!

CONGREGATION: Christ the Lord is risen indeed! Alleluia!

(Reader 2 should light the Paschal candle and encourage everyone to ring their bells. Other readers should sprinkle water onto the group as an act of celebration and baptismal remembrance.)

In closing, lead in singing "Christ the Lord Is Risen Today" or another Easter hymn.

THE BENEDICTION

READER 2: Go forth into the world to proclaim the good news of our risen Lord!

READER 3: Go forth into the world, submitting yourself to the King of life, who has conquered death!

READER 4: Go forth into the world with the light of Christ!

READER 1: Go forth into the world, bending joyful footsteps and hearts to our God!

Starters

1 Jesus said,

"I am the bread of life."

"Whoever comes to me will never be hungry, and whoever believes in me will never be thirsty" (John 6:35).

Lord Jesus, satisfy our longing. Feed our souls. We come; we believe. We sit at your table. Amen.

2 Jesus said,

"I am the light of the world."

"Whoever follows me will never walk in darkness but will have the light of life" (John 8:12).

Lord Jesus, guide our steps. Keep us from the dark places. We want to walk with you. Amen.

3 Jesus said,

"I am the gate."

"Whoever enters by me will be saved.... I came that they may have life, and have it abundantly" (John 10:9-10).

Lord Jesus, open the gate to our hearts and come inside. Save us from ourselves; save us for the abundant life you offer. We enter with thanksgiving. Amen.

4 Jesus said,

"I am the good shepherd."

"I know my own and my own know me, just as the Father knows me and I know the Father" (John 10:14-15).

Lord Jesus, keep us always in your care. Let us not wander from your love. We want to be with you; we want to know you as our own. Amen.

5 Jesus said,

"I am the resurrection and the life."

"Those who believe in me, even though they die, will live, and everyone who lives and believes in me will never die" (John 11:25-26).

Lord Jesus, I believe. Please help my unbelief and give me hope to start again. Let my belief give way to faith and faith give way to trust and trust give way to life. Give me life, Lord. Amen.

6 Jesus said,

"I am the way, and the truth, and the life."

"No one comes to the Father except through me. If you know me, you will know my Father also" (John 14:6-7a).

Lord Jesus, bless us with a glimpse of our glorious Maker. Show us the way of peace, the truth of love, the life everlasting. We choose your path. Amen.

7 Jesus said,

"I am the vine, you are the branches."

"Those who abide in me and I in them bear much fruit, because apart from me you can do nothing" (John 15:5).

Lord Jesus, flow through us. Keep us rooted in you that we may bear fruit that pleases you and that nourishes the hungry around us. We live to serve in your name. Amen.

Jesus Prayer

| Am | Am | G | F | F | Am | Am | B♭ | B♭ | |

Lord Jesus Christ, Son of God,   have mercy on me a sinner.

| Am | Am | G | F | F | Am | Am | B♭ | F | C |

Lord Jesus Christ, Son of God,   have mercy on me a sinner.

Words and music by Jenny Youngman
© 2007 Jenny Youngman

Doxology

| B | | | E | B | | E | |

Praise God the fountain of blessings.   We lift our voice in praise.

| B | | | E | B | | E | |

Praise God the Three in One,   the Father, Spirit, and Son.

| B | | | E | F#sus | F# | B | |

Praise God the fountain of blessings.   We lift our voice in praise.

Words and Music by Jenny Youngman
© 2007 Jenny Youngman

Worship You

Verse 1
C   G   Am   G
Worship you, I worship you in all I say and all I do,

  F   Gsus G   C
With all my life, O Lord, I worship you.

Verse 2
C   G   Am   G
Praise you, Lord, I'll praise you, Lord, with all my heart, with all my voice.

  Am   Gsus G   C
With all I am, O Lord, I'll praise you.

Chorus
  F   Gsus   G   C   F   Gsus G   Gsus
It is my life,   but it is yours. I lay it down. I lay it down.

G   F   Gsus   G   C   F   Gsus   G
It is your cross,   but it is mine. I take it up. I take it up.

Verse 3
C   G   Am   G
Serve you, Lord, I'll serve you, Lord. My hands and feet are yours alone.

  F   Gsus G   C
My humble vow to you, I'll serve you.

Words and music by Jenny Youngman
© 2007 Jenny Youngman

C   G   Am   F   Gsus

On Our Way

G   F   C   C   F   G   F   C   C

Verse 1
C   F   F   C
I gave my burden to the Lord—repented of my sin,

   C   F   F   C
And went to face temptation in the Wilderness of Zin.

   C   F   F   C
The tempter asked me if I could be faithful even when the stakes got high,

   C   F   F   C
So I grabbed my staff, put my sandals on, and left my bags behind.

Chorus
   G   F   C   C   F   G   F   C   C
I'm on   my way.   I'm on   my way.

Verse 2
   C   F   F   C
The teacher found me working on the Sea of Galilee;

   C   F   F   C
He waved to me from the shore and called me to follow where he'd lead.

Chorus
   G   F   C   C   F   G   F   C   C
I'm on   my way.   I'm on   my way.

Verse 3
   C   F   F   C
I let him into my home and my heart, and I listened to him teach;

Words and music by Josh Tinley
© 2007 Josh Tinley

```
    :C              :F      :F          :C
```
And then I emptied my alabaster jar upon his feet.

Chorus
```
    :G    :F    :C    :C  F    :G    :F    :C        :C
```
I'm on   my way.   I'm on   my way.

```
F        :Em      :Dm      :C        :F        :Em      :Dm      :C        :
```

Bridge
```
    :F                  :Em        :Dm            :C
```
The Son of Man will be handed over, betrayed into human hands;

```
    :F              :Em        :Dm          :C
```
The soldiers of the governor will kill him on commands;

```
    :F              :Em          :Dm          :C
```
The one who gave us hope will hang in shame upon a hill.

```
        :F          :Em        :Dm        :C              :
```
But if we suffer this injustice, we will realize God's will.

```
G        :F      :C      :C  F    :G        :F      :C      :C        :
```

Verse 4
```
    :C                  :F              :F          :C
```
A couple days went by, and then I went to see his grave.

```
    :C                          :F          :F              :C
```
But the tomb wasn't sealed: The stone had moved to reveal a shroud and an empty cave.

Chorus
```
    :G    :F    :C    :C  F    :G    :F    :C        :C
```
I'm on   my way.   I'm on   my way.

Chorus
```
    :G    :F    :C  :C  F    :G    :F        :C      :C
```
We're on   our way.   We're on   our way.

Repeat last chorus and fade

G   F   C   Em   Dm

Carry Your Cross

Verse 1

Em   Bm   C   D

I'll follow you, I'll follow you, I'll follow you and you alone.

Em   Bm   C   D   Em   F

I'll praise your name, I'll praise your name, I'll praise your name, O Lord.

Chorus

G   C   Am   D   G   C   Am   G

   Will you carry your cross   and trust in me when hope seems lost?

G   C   Am   D   G   C   Am   D

   Will you lose yourself and follow me?

Verse 2

Em   Bm   C   D

   I'll give my life, I'll give my life, I'll give my life—I'll give it all.

Em   Bm   C   D   Em   F

   I'll do your will, I'll do your will, I'll do your will, O God.

Repeat Chorus

Chorus (modified)

G   C   Am   D   G   C   Am   G

   I will carry my cross   and trust in you when hope seems lost.

G   C   Am   D   G   C   Am   D

   I will lose myself and follow you.

Chorus (modified again)

G   C   Am   D   G   C   Am   G

   We will carry our cross   and trust in you when hope seems lost.

G   C   Am   D   G   C   Am   D

   We will lose ourselves and follow you.

Words and music by Josh Tinley
© 2007 Josh Tinley

Em   Bm   C   D   F   G   Am